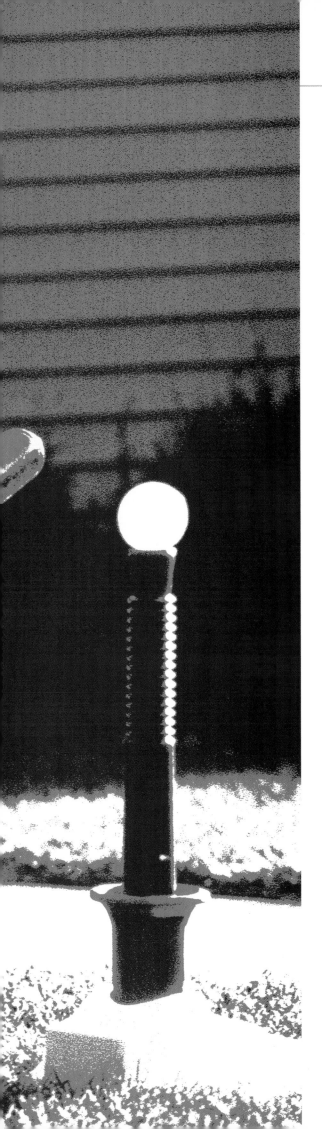

Fathers
&Sons

Stories of how sport builds lifelong bonds

Presented by Beckett Publications

Published by: Beckett Publications

15850 Dallas Parkway

Dallas, TX 75248

Beckett® is a registered trademark of Beckett Publications.

This book is not licensed, authorized or endorsed by any individual,

player, league or players association.

First Edition: March 1999

Beckett Corporate Sales and Information (972) 991-6657

CONTENTS

Grant (Hill) got from his father what Calvin's dad told him: "The difference between a pat on the back and a kick in the behind is about 18 inches, and I'm gonna do both."

Sometimes, in spite of all the things you do wrong, (children) show you something greater in them, something surprising that lets you know they're going to be all right.

FIRST HEROES

By Kevin Sherrington

Field of Dreams is not a movie about baseball. Kevin Costner didn't have to be an Iowa farmer. He could have been an owner who razes a perfectly good stadium and builds one with 70,000 luxury boxes. Suite Dreams, he could have called it.

And we'd still love it.

We'd love it for the same reasons we love Field of Dreams. And that's not so much because Costner pulled Shoeless Joe out of the corn or coaxed a bushel of corn out of Burt Lancaster.

Face it: The movie's not all that good. Costner is about as wooden as the bats. His wife is almost as loony as the premise, which is that this farmer hears a Voice. The Voice used to work the game-show circuit, whispering, "The password is . . . aardvark," in a tone so conspiratorial it's as if he's giving you J. Edgar Hoover's home phone number. Or his dress size, maybe.

But talk shows replaced game shows, so the disembodied Voice goes to Iowa to haunt Kevin Costner, who right away realizes this is not Password or Iowa, either. Anyway, the movie has its rough spots. And it doesn't matter.

It doesn't matter because of the last five minutes, when Kevin Costner finally gets in the game and pitches the best line: "Dad," he asks, tentatively, a little boy scared to hope for too much, "wanna have a catch?"

This gets us every time. Fathers and sons. We never tire of these stories.

We want to know if Ken Griffey Jr. always wore his cap backwards when he was growing up in the clubhouse around his father and the Big Red Machine. What did Brett Hull learn all those years hanging around the ice, when he was the hyper cub of the Golden Jet? And Peyton Manning's touch of class: Did he acquire it on his own or was it passed down from Archie?

Genes are a funny thing. Mickey Mantle had four sons. A couple looked just like him. The closest any of them came to the major leagues was when they stood next to the old man in the family photo. Bobby Valentine's dad? Tiny. Doak Walker's? Scholarly.

And then every couple hundred thousand athletes, you get a Grant Hill, the son of a great athlete in his own right, Calvin

9

Hill. But it takes more than genes, too. Grant got from his father what Calvin's dad told him: "The difference between a pat on the back and a kick in the behind is about 18 inches, and I'm gonna do both for you."

Grant got the best of everything: A football hero for a father, a man educated at Yale, who has worked in business and with professional teams in both baseball and football, a man able to give his only child things most fathers can't.

And the most valuable thing he gave him was his time.

Calvin recently sent some friends the results of a study showing the impact of fathers on sons. "Family structure," he said, "was more important than income and all the other things we tend to consider when trying to figure out what's best for our children."

Calvin had that structure when he was growing up, the son of a construction worker.

"Your father was your first hero," he said. "Every once in a while, we'd go by a building and my father would say he built that, and I'd think he did it single-handedly. I'd think he must be pretty important. And, because he loved me, I must be pretty important, too."

People figure because Grant has done so well that Calvin has reason to be proud. Talking to a group of recovering

addicts in a prison, Hill heard an inmate ask what it felt like to watch his son dunk a basketball in the NCAA Championship game.

Calvin told him it was great, a natural high, exactly what the men in the prison expected. And then he told them something they didn't expect.

"It was no different from the feeling I had when he was born, or when he took his first step, or went off to school the first day. Most of you guys have children and you're not in touch with them. That's what you're missing."

Many times, maybe more often than not, Dad doesn't get it right. Terrell Davis' father once measured the courage of his sons by lining them up against a wall and firing shots over their heads.

You don't have to risk your son's life to screw it up, either. For Rick Barry's kids, the harm came in the criticism he always had for the way they played basketball. That and his absence led Barry's boys to credit their mom for the success they've enjoyed in professional basketball.

Lots of dads go over the top. You see these kinds of fathers all the time. Guys who scream at their sons for missing a pass or blowing a play. Guys who won't let their sons come in for dinner until they make a hundred free throws.

I once wrote a story about just such a kid. His father and uncles had been great high school and college basketball players. He was good, too, the best player on the only team that beat Shaquille O'Neal's high school team.

But the kid gave up on basketball before he had to.

He never said why. He wouldn't talk about it at all, not even with his old teammates. He didn't need to. They knew what it was like, growing up in that house, under the weight of all those expectations.

You see this father all the time. Maybe you see him in the mirror. He doesn't mean to be a jerk, but he wants his kid to be great, wants him to be something he wasn't. And he can't understand why the kid doesn't want it as much as he does.

Most great athletes never put that on their kids. They know how hard it is. You grow up the son of Cal Ripken Jr. or Mark McGwire, and the first thing everyone wants to know is if you're as good as your father.

Does the kid show the stuff of a Hall of Famer? Who does?

Tom Grieve was just an average player. But he knew his youngest son, Ben, was special from the first time he swung a bat at the age of 2. Still, he didn't push too hard. He taught Ben how to play the game, but Tom believes most of what Ben absorbed came from hanging around a major league clubhouse.

John Elway learned everything from his father, Jack. He taught him how to throw, how to read a defense, how to handle himself.

Doug Flutie never will teach his son to throw a pass. Dougie is 7. Four years ago, he suddenly stopped talking, and doctors diagnosed him with autism. Doug Flutie doesn't hope that one day his son will throw a famous pass, as he did.

Doug doesn't think much past today, when he wakes up in the morning and hopes, maybe, his son will say, "I love you." Most days, Dad settles for a smile so quick, so small that only he recognizes it.

A father-son relationship is hard to figure sometimes. One of Bob Knight's sons played for him at Indiana. You

remember Pat. He was the son that the old man once kicked at on the bench. You probably don't remember the picture from Pat's last game at Indiana. Father and son are embracing. You can't see Pat's face, but you can see Bob's, at least the part that isn't buried in Pat's shoulder. He's crying.

Bob called Pat his "all-time favorite player." A few years later, Pat returned the compliment. He told a radio station in Green Bay that, if he had only one day to live, he'd want to spend it with his father.

Maybe it helps to have understanding children.

One thing all fathers have in common, famous or not, is that they make mistakes with their sons. I brought this up once while interviewing Chan Gailey, not long after he was named coach of the Cowboys. He had a reputation of dealing fairly with players, and I wanted to see if there was a time when he wasn't.

I did it by asking him about regrets. I told him about something that had happened at my house that morning, how I'd been too harsh with my oldest son, Jake, and had regretted it all day.

A few minutes later, after the interview was over and he had left the room, he walked back in.

"You know," he said, softly, one father to another, "it'll be all right. They always forget."

I don't know. I do know this: There is nothing more humbling than the forgiveness of a child.

Jake, who is 7, the same age as Doug Flutie's son, always says the same thing when I apologize for some transgression: "That's all right, Dad."

No, it isn't, I tell him. But I appreciate it just the same.

I have coached Jake in soccer and baseball. I expect I will do the same with his brother, Ford. I don't know what it will be like coaching the younger one, or if I will have the same expectations.

I hope not. Jake set a high standard. I remember the first time I saw his best quality on a sports field — his great heart.

We were at a rodeo in a small North Texas town. Sometime between the steer wrestling and team roping, swatting at bugs that come from miles to buzz the lights poking into the darkness, parents send their children down to the red dirt floor for the calf scramble.

No one catches a calf at these things. The idea is everyone has a good time trying and, after hapless lunges and tumbles, the hundred or so children return to their seats, dirtier and happier.

All do that except one — a flop-haired 4-year-old boy who won't give up on the calf. On and on the boy runs, never getting any closer to the prize than when

he started. He won't stop until we send somebody out to get him.

Children are funny. They carry your genes and your hopes, so already they start out with two strikes against them. But, sometimes, in spite of all the things you do wrong, they show you something greater in them, something surprising that lets you know they're going to be all right.

On those occasions, sitting in the bleachers watching a little boy chase a calf, I am no different from Archie Manning or Jack Elway or Calvin Hill.

We are all just fathers. Proud fathers.

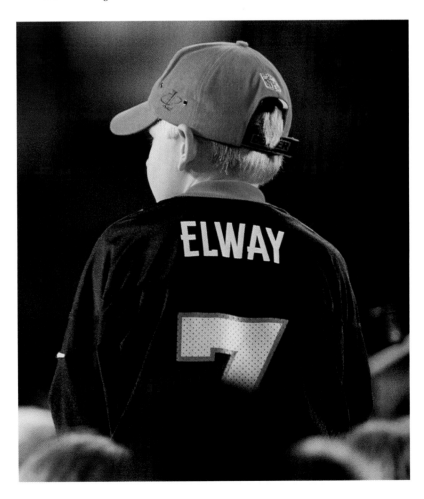

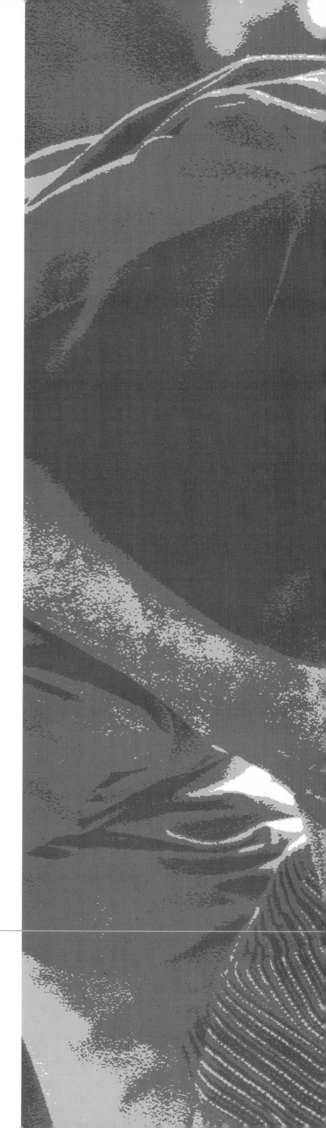

"I guess I owe (my dad) a huge debt of gratitude. Some people get their competitiveness from their brothers or friends. I got it from my dad."

— *Grant Hill*

"(My son) knows what his dad has done, but he just knows me as a dad. And that's the most important thing."

— *Mark McGwire*

PERSPECTIVE

By Chris McCosky

Calvin Hill, a former NFL All-Pro running back with the Cowboys, Browns and Redskins, and his son, Grant, have made their own marks in sports. A forward with the Detroit Pistons, Grant is a four-time NBA All-Star and a 1996 Olympic gold medal winner.

Many kids feel the need to follow in their father's footsteps. Grant Hill spent most of his life trying to travel a path to even greater success.

That's no small task when you consider his father is Calvin Hill, a respected Yale grad and All-Pro running back for the Dallas Cowboys, Cleveland Browns and Washington Redskins in the 1960s and '70s.

"My dad would always say to me, 'Remember, you only have half of my chromosomes. So as good as you are, I am twice as good,'" recalls Grant, who also received a healthy dose of talent-laden DNA from his mother, Janet, an attorney and well-respected consultant in the Washington, D.C., area.

Grant's recounting of his dad's favorite line speaks volumes about their relationship. The simple fact Grant remembers the statement illustrates its impact on him as a kid. The words paint a life-size picture of father and son's loving, yet intensely competitive, relationship. An inch was never given or expected.

"I think because I didn't have any brothers or sisters, none of the usual sibling rivalries that most kids have, my rivalry was always with my father," Grant says.

"Rivalry" has the ring of understatement, considering the intensity of their backyard battles.

From the time Grant was in the first grade, the two would play basketball, one-on-one, at the Hill house in Reston, Va. Calvin would show no mercy. Not once did he let young Grant win. Finally, when Grant was 15, he beat his father.

Calvin never played him again.

"I guess I owe him a huge debt of gratitude, though," Grant says. "As I got older, I became obsessed with trying to differentiate myself from what he had done. That's what drove me. Some people get their competitiveness from their brothers or friends. I got it from my dad."

It wasn't always a pleasant struggle.

Grant remembers with horror the day the famous Calvin Hill came to speak to his eighth grade class. Grant faked an illness and stayed in the school's sick room.

"I never wanted any of the other kids to think that I thought I was better than anybody, just because my dad was a pro athlete," Grant explains. "I just wanted to fit in."

Grant jokes that for the first 15 years of his life, he thought his full name actually was, "Grant Hill, Son of. . . ."

"No matter what I accomplished, my title was 'Son of Ex-NFL Star Calvin Hill,'" Grant says. "I used to say, 'Why do you guys always have to say something about my dad? When he was playing, you never mentioned my name.'"

To make a name for himself, Grant

fought hard to extricate himself from his father's shadow. His dad played football, so he played basketball and soccer. His dad's personality could best be described as intense, so Grant went out of his way to be laid back. His dad prided himself on rigorous pregame preparation and focus, so Grant steadfastly refused any such regimen.

"Before a game I might be juggling a soccer ball or playing in the streets," Grant says. "My dad would ask, 'Aren't you going to lie down, put your feet up?' If the game was at 7:30, I might not leave the house until 6. It drove him crazy. Because he prepared so hard, I wanted him to think it all came easy to me."

But as much as he rebelled with an ongoing game of one-upmanship, he acknowledges now that he has turned out to be very much like Calvin, at least in terms of his professional life.

Grant became an All-American at Duke, helping to lead the Blue Devils to a pair of NCAA championships. He's now a perennial All-Star forward with the Detroit Pistons and is lauded for his work ethic, intelligence and consistency.

"Everything about me now, as far as basketball, came from him: My competitiveness, the way I take my job seriously, my personality, the way I handle certain things," Grant says. "It's him."

W hile in high school Kobe regularly played one-on-one with his father, Joe "Jelly Bean" Bryant, who played eight seasons in the NBA. Those games and his dad's advice helped the Lakers' guard become the youngest All-Star in NBA history. "My father always played with a great love for the game, and that's one thing he always taught me," Kobe said about his childhood. "He told me not to let the pressure or the expectations take away from my love of the game. I think that's the best advice anyone has ever given me."

Emotionally charged by his son, Matt, Cardinals first baseman Mark McGwire exploded to hit 70 home runs in 1998. Before the season, his son — a part-time Cards batboy — requested 65 homers. Dad never revealed if Matt increased his order to 70.

You didn't have to be a baseball fan to savor the father and son sports moment of the decade.

Mark McGwire of the St. Louis Cardinals had just hit his 61st home run, tying Roger Maris's big-league record for a single season. As the 6-foot-5, 250-pound red-haired giant touched home plate, he was met by his batboy son, 10-year-old Matt. Rather than high-five the lad, McGwire hoisted him overhead and delivered a Hall of Fame hug.

The moment was made even more poignant by details that came out later. Matt, who lives in Southern California with Mark's ex-wife, Kathy Williamson, flew to St. Louis for that afternoon game. The boy did not arrive at the ballpark until 45 minutes before the first pitch.

"I didn't see him there in the top of the first inning," McGwire said after the game. "Then, when I went into the hole to get my bat, there he is. I told him I loved him, gave him a kiss. The next thing I knew, I saw him at home plate."

That was after McGwire had turned the third pitch from Chicago Cubs pitcher Mike Morgan into a 430-foot rocket that slammed off a window in the Stadium Club in left field at Busch Stadium.

As young Matt led the celebration at home plate, McGwire said to himself, "What a wonderful feeling for a father to have."

That line also applied to McGwire's dad, John, seated behind home plate on his 61st birthday. Mark had not been able to call his dad with birthday greetings before the game.

"If this is meant to be," McGwire told himself en route to the ballyard, "to give him this birthday present, this 61st home-run on his 61st birthday, so be it."

McGwire marveled when he recalled that feeling at his post-game press conference. "It just happened to be," he said. "So happy birthday, Dad!"

The next day, Sept. 8, 1998, Mark and Matt relived a once-in-a-lifetime dream for all fathers and sons. Dad passed Maris with homer No. 62, a 340-foot blur that just cleared the left field fence.

Dad and kid exchanged no words during their two uplifting moments at home plate. "He didn't have to say anything," McGwire said. "His eyes said it all."

Later, McGwire recalled, "He was laughing the whole time. I said, 'What do you think of that?' He said 'Well, you put me waaay up there!'"

McGwire knew that his own life was changed forever, and he could accept that inescapable fact. He was disturbed to find out the same fate involved his son.

When Matt returned to elementary school in Southern California, a tabloid television show tried to film the boy on campus. Dad, naturally, was outraged.

"He's a 10-year-old," McGwire said. "Allow him to be a child. Allow him to go to school. What his father does doesn't mean he's more special than anyone else. He knows what his dad has done, but he just knows me as a dad. And that's the most important thing."

Even half a continent away, Matt remained part of his father's march to a home run total that a mere months before seemed absurd, if not impossible: 70.

On Sept. 20 in Milwaukee, dad conked No. 65 in the first inning off left-hander Scott Karl. When McGwire reached home plate, he paused to chat with teammate Brian Jordan, the next hitter.

"I was telling him about my son," McGwire said. "I don't think anybody knew about it."

The secret McGwire revealed to Jordan was a preseason request from the son to the father.

"I asked him how many home runs he wanted his dad to hit," McGwire recalled. "He looked me in the eye and said, 'Sixty-five.'"

That was four more than anyone had hit in 37 years. Was dad surprised?

"Yeah," McGwire said. "Wouldn't you be? But that's all I thought about when I was running around the bases. That ball means a lot to me. I hope I get it back."

What would he do with it?

"I'll give it to my son," McGwire bellowed. "I mean, what a prediction. My God!"

(The ball was returned by Charles Dombrowski, 21, a college senior, in exchange for autographed items and an audience with McGwire.)

Someone asked after that game for Mark's reaction if Matt were to call and up the ante to 70 homers. "I'll have to sit him down," McGwire replied.

Seventy homers it was.

Skeptics should not doubt that McGwire's first allegiance is to Matt, not some home run derby. In fact, this father's devotion to his son predated the boy's birth.

Kathy was due to deliver Matt on the last day of the 1987 season. McGwire, then with the Oakland Athletics, had 49 home runs, already the major league record for a rookie. With another homer, the father-to-be would become the 12th big leaguer to hit 50. McGwire never hesitated. He took the day off to be with his wife for the birth of their son.

Father and son remain close, due in large part because the parental split was so amiable. Mark lives five minutes away from Matt, and they see each other often, even during the season when dad is 1,500 miles away.

McGwire signed with the Cardinals in 1997 for less than market value, but he had two non-negotiable demands, which the club happily met. Whenever Matt can make a road trip, he always has a seat on the team plane. And whenever he watches dad play, he can do so as batboy.

That's how Mark and Matt came to meet at home plate on that historic September day and provide us with that rarest of moments: how fathers and sons ought to be.

"I saw how . . . he handled the fans and how he handled the media and how he did it with a lot of class. I certainly learned a lot from my dad."

— *Peyton Manning*

"I learn a lot from (my dad) even now, on a daily basis, just by watching him. How you act around a ballpark. How you talk to the players. How you ask questions."

— *Joe Buck*

FATHER LIKE SON

Peyton Manning considers himself fortunate to have grown up as the son of an NFL quarterback.

He didn't feel pressure to perform up to the high standards set by his dad, Archie, who played 13 seasons with New Orleans, Houston and Minnesota and is still a legend in the Cresent City.

Peyton didn't feel the need to rebel in an effort to forge his own identity as an individual and an athlete.

One part of him, the kid, simply had fun hanging around his father's teammates and hanging out with his dad. Another part of him watched and learned what it takes to be a professional athlete. That part, the student, laid the foundation for a career that promises to make him the best quarterback in the family.

If Peyton didn't brag to his dad about being the No. 1 overall pick in the 1998 NFL draft, the Colts' signal caller could boast about being Offensive Rookie of the Year. Archie didn't achieve either one, and his son couldn't care less. More dear to Peyton than his achievements are his childhood memories of being a son of Archie Manning.

"I was 8 when dad retired in 1984," Peyton recalls. "I can remember hanging around the Saints' locker room after games and playing football with my older brother Cooper in the Superdome.

An icon in New Orleans' sports history, Archie Manning was a Pro Bowl quarterback during his career with the Saints from 1971 to 1982. His son Payton earned 1998 NFL Offensive Rookie of the Year honors and was the only quarterback in the NFL to take every snap for his team.

We would roll up a ball of tape — that would be our football — and we'd play one-on-one on that 100-yard turf. First one to score won, because we'd be out of breath.

"Afterward, we'd be ready to go home. But dad would be doing all these interviews and signing all these autographs. We'd say, 'C'mon dad, let's go, let's go.' He'd hear us, but he'd keep doing his job — signing the autographs and doing the interviews.

"I can certainly appreciate that now. I have friends in town for games, whether at the University of Tennessee or Indianapolis, or my girlfriend might say, 'Hey Peyton let's go.' And I'll say, 'Hey now, this is part of my job. I got to do my interviews and I got to sign these autographs for the fans.'

"Even as I got older, I saw how he handled situations during his last few years and immediately after he stopped playing. How he handled the fans and how he handled the media and how he did it with a lot of class.

I certainly learned a lot from my dad."

Even at the tender age of 3, Peyton knew a lot about football. He knew the names of his dad's receivers and running backs by heart. But unlike most kids, Peyton never asked for autographs. Instead, he shook hands.

"We were football fanatics even at a young age," Peyton says. "It was a different way to grow up because I got to meet a lot of neat people as a kid. I loved sports and I loved football at an early age. All of us did. Just getting a chance to meet the Saints' players and the different players that my dad knew around the league, it was a neat way to grow up.

"We were always big Wes Chandler fans. He was one of my dad's top receivers. And then Stan Brock. I liked him. Everybody loved Rickey Jackson. Rickey and Stan were the guys who were still there when we were kind of old enough to know what was going on. Then, in 1979, I went to the Pro Bowl with my dad and got to meet Walter Payton and Roger Staubach.

"Those were fun moments. Of course, my dad was always my favorite player."

While other friends pretended they were Joe Montana or Roger Staubach, Peyton always pretended to be his dad.

"We always got different kinds of equipment for Christmas, either shoulder pads or uniforms or things like that," Peyton recalls. "We'd always go out and play on Christmas day. My dad would film it and we would watch it the next day. We still have those tapes. There's a lot of classic footage on those tapes.

"He'd say, 'Do your five-step drop.' I had a nerf ball and I'd kind of waddle

back. I was a chubby kid. I was 3 years old. I say I remembered it, but a lot of it is on videotape. I have the pictures in my head, doing my five-step drop and throwing it out there. If Cooper would tackle me too hard, I'd go complain to my dad. You never see my dad on film, because he's always filming."

After Saints games, Archie would come home full of aches and pains and ask his sons to help ease the hurt.

"Dad used to trick us," Peyton recalls. "He had Cooper and I competing over who could give the best massage. He'd say, 'Cooper, you go 20 minutes. And Peyton, you go 20 minutes. And I'll tell you who's best. And we'll have a playoff.'

"That was the thing about dad. He

always tried to make things fun for us. He never pushed us into sports, never at all. The only thing he did say was, 'If you're going to do something, though, you need to give it your best effort. And you need to finish it.' That was important.

"If you were going to commit to a team, you needed to give your very best effort and work hard at it. Just like he'd say the same thing for school. We always tried to do our best at that."

All three boys born to Olivia and Archie Manning have followed in their father's footsteps.

The oldest, Cooper, a wide receiver, went on to the University of Mississippi, his father's alma mater, where a back injury ended his career. Peyton was allowed to stay in the family after breaking tradition, but not the bloodlines, by going to Tennessee. The youngest, Eli, also a quarterback, starred at Newman High School in New Orleans and in fall 1999 will continue the family tradition at Ole Miss.

Archie encouraged them to play sports, but he didn't demand it or expect it. Rather, he made it difficult for his sons not to enjoy playing baseball or football or any other sport.

"My dad never coached Little League," Peyton says. "Other people always coached us. But he was at all our games. He video-taped us a lot. He'd throw the baseball around and do the little things. But he always made it a lot of fun.

"That's what I remember. That's why I think all of us loved sports so much, because he made it fun for us growing up. You see a lot of kids play the sport their dad played because their dad is pushing them."

Not everything Archie and Peyton did together was fun.

"The one time he did try to coach me didn't work out," Peyton says. "I was about 9 years old when he coached my basket-ball team. We had 10 players on our team and I was the top player. But he drafted all of his friends' sons, and they were the worst players in the league, and we went like 2-8. We were awful. I was mad."

Other than that debacle, Archie stayed in the background.

"He was always just a fan, always in the stands," Peyton remembers. "I think he just wanted to be a parent. But he was at all the games and videotaped the games. He never said anything, never ever tried to get involved with the coach. He'd never tell him how to do something.

"He thought it was more important for him and my mother to sit in the stands and be supportive like most of the other parents."

It appears dad was right, and Peyton will always appreciate that.

W hen Cal Ripken Jr. signs autographs, he adds a "Jr." tail as a tribute to his father, Cal Ripken Sr., who spent more than 30 years with the Baltimore Orioles as a player, third base coach and manager, and in 1987 became the first father to manage two sons — Cal and Billy — simultaneously.

"(My dad) not only taught me the fundamentals of the game of baseball, but he also taught me to play it the right way, and to play it the Oriole way," Ripken said the night he broke Lou Gehrig's record for consecutive games played. "From the beginning, my dad let me know how important it was to be there for your team and to be counted on by your teammates."

hen Hale Irwin isn't raking in millions on the Senior PGA Tour, he's giving tips to his son, Steven, at events such as the PGA Father/Son Challenge in December at Vero Beach, Fla. The Irwin kids grew up in Frontenac, Mo., in the house Hale and his wife, Sally, purchased in the early 1970s just before Hale's career took off with his victory in the 1974 U.S. Open. Steve has competed on the NIKE Tour, light years away from his dad's accomplishments: three U.S. Open titles and nearly $8 million in winnings in 3-1/2 years on the Senior Tour.

ack Buck, the Hall of Fame voice of the St. Louis Cardinals, has been in the team's broadcast booth since 1954. His son, Joe, sits beside him now as heir apparent and the young star of the Fox network.

It seems like a natural pairing, but Joe, now 30, wasn't destined to share air time with his dad.

"One of my earliest memories was when I was maybe 3 years old," Joe recalls. "I was in the back of the Cardinal broadcast booth at Busch Stadium. My dad and Mike Shannon were down there in front of me in the first row. I was watching the game with my mom, and the Cardinals scored a run early in the game, and I got excited. And I knocked a cup of Coke down on my dad and Shannon.

"They obviously weren't expecting it. They shot up out of their chairs — still doing the call — and whipped around with a look on their faces like, 'Who did that!'

"Their first thought wasn't that it was Jack's little son Joe. So they spun around with these nasty looks on their faces, and it was one of the scariest moments of my young life.

"And I started crying. When they realized what happened, they calmed me down and got me to laugh about it. But it

Jack Buck and his son, Joe, have combined talents on St. Louis Cardinals radio broadcasts since 1991. A part of Cardinals radio since 1954, Jack Buck is a member of the Broadcasters' Hall of Fame, the Radio Hall of Fame and the Baseball Hall of Fame.

wasn't much fun for them, either. It was a hot, sticky, St. Louis summer day. And they had to do the rest of the game with Coca-Cola all over them.

"It was like the first Gatorade drenching. Little did I know that 17 years later, I'd be doing the game with them."

Joe joined the Cardinals' broadcast team in 1991. He once bristled when critics used the term "nepotism" to describe his precocious career.

"Going to the broadcast booth was as comfortable to me as going to the kitchen at home," Joe says. "When I was a kid, I went to the booth every day with my dad. I was in the locker room every day, watching my dad and taking grief from the players. The stuff I learned, you can't read about and you can't get anywhere else.

"Now, when people say it's nepotism, well, it's true! I was doing Cardinal games when I was 19. What other 19-year-old is going to get that opportunity, unless they're somebody's kid?"

Joe pegs his success to the example set by his father, now 74 and cutting back because of Parkinson's Disease.

"I was always fascinated by my dad and watching him work," Joe explains. "I was kind of transfixed by what he was doing and the people he was around. That's how the whole thing got rolling.

It's something I always knew I wanted to do, and it's something I knew I would do. It was just a matter of when. I learn a lot from him even now, on a daily basis, just by watching him. How you act around a ballpark. How you talk to the players. How you ask questions."

Being a junior partner, so to speak, in the old man's firm can be an ordeal. Not for the Bucks. They have always cherished their time together, which was limited by Jack's travel schedule.

"That's the best thing about it, getting to work with him now," Joe says. "Growing up, my dad was in and out of town, obviously. When he was in town, it was like two guys hanging out, rather than a father and a son. I was a guy who could always make him laugh, and he was the funniest guy I'd ever met. He did his best to see every baseball game, every football game, I played in. But it was not a go-to-your-room-you're-grounded type of father-son relationship.

"Now, when we're in the booth, he's good for me. And I try to help keep him young. And you know what? There has never been a moment of friction between us. It's strange, I know. But I look forward every day to working with him. To me, it's the perfect way to make up for all the travelling he did when I was a kid. Now I'm a young adult who gets to work with my dad. Most guys do it the other way.

Their dad was around when they were young, then they grow up and move away.

"I prefer it this way, as a person now capable of understanding what he's all about. I cherish these times, because I know this isn't going to last forever. I'm getting a lot of time back in our relationship."

The job training never stops, even as Joe's star rises over the national scene.

"When you work with somebody," Joe says, "it's impossible not to pick up little characteristics and traits. The best part is that with him, whatever I pick up, it's something I want to pick up. Technical broadcast stuff, like his pacing. Or the difference between doing a radio game and TV game.

"But he's taught me even more about how to act as a human being. And not to think that being a broadcaster puts you on a higher standing than anyone else. There are a lot of people who would kill to have these jobs. So have fun with it, and don't take yourself too seriously."

That's why Joe, who left Indiana University to become a minor league play-by-play man, can shrug off the nepotism comments. He knows the hard work that went into his apprenticeship. As his father has demonstrated for four decades, the best weapon against critics is self-deprecating humor.

"When I was 14 or 15," Joe recalls, "I'd go to Busch Stadium and do the game into a tape recorder in an empty booth. I sent the tape to get the Louisville job in 1989. Then it was a challenge to get the Cardinal job, but people here were fair and ready to give me a chance. It went well. It could very easily have swung the other way.

"And let's face it, once you get established in a town like this, it's hard to mess it up. It's a Supreme Court Justice type of thing. You're in for life."

Since he's in the booth with his dad, Joe's also having the time of his life.

"I finally understand several of the things that (my dad) has been speaking about all of my life. I feel like we are able to relate to each other a lot easier."

— *Dale Earnhardt Jr.*

"The great thing is, (my dad) knows exactly what you're talking about. He's been through exactly the same thing."

— *Brett Hull*

CONNECTIONS

A seven-time **NASCAR** **Winston Cup** champion, Dale Earnhardt is a **NASCAR** living legend with more than $33 million in career earnings and 71 victories. His son, Dale Jr., came into his own in 1998, winning the Busch title.

Dale Earnhardt Jr.'s fondest childhood memories center on racing. Of course, that would be expected from someone whose grandfather and father were both named to NASCAR's list of 50 greatest drivers, and from someone who recently made the Earnhardts the first family to have three generations of drivers win NASCAR titles.

Grandfather Ralph Earnhardt tore up the short tracks in North Carolina, plus won a NASCAR Sportsman title.

Daddy Dale Earnhardt captured a record-tying seven Winston Cup champions and the 1998 Daytona 500.

Dale Jr. — who goes by "Junior" or "Little E" — won the 1998 Busch Grand National in a car owned by his father.

Ask Junior about his favorite Christmases, and he replies, "I guess the best times were when I was a little kid. It's hard to beat a slot-car track or a bunch of cars to play with when you're 6 or 7."

When he talks about his favorite vacation, he describes the July race in Daytona. Not only did he get to go to the races, but also to the beach.

But while racing is a family sport, the demands of a Winston Cup career and superstardom can shortchange a father-son relationship. Throw in a divorce and the normal growing pains of a teenager, and the bonds can even be strained.

"One of the biggest questions of my career has been about my relationship and growing up as Dale Earnhardt's son," Junior says. "There were times when the demands of my dad were overwhelming.

"Sometimes we felt like we had been cheated out of the things that normal kids do with their dads like soccer games and school activities. But it all made sense every time dad won a race or a championship."

Things make even more sense when you join the family business. Especially when your daddy makes you learn it from

the ground up, starting off with sweeping out the shop.

Junior enjoyed the benefits of his father's name and money. He has raced his entire career in cars owned by his father.

But his father also demanded more of his son than his other employees.

"We've gotten a lot closer," Junior says, "just because I'm starting to go through some of the things he's had to go through during his career. And I'm understanding him more.

"I finally understand several of the things that he has been speaking about all of my life. I feel like we are able to relate to each other a lot easier."

Dale Sr. didn't earn nicknames such as "The Man in Black" and "The Intimidator" by being a sensitive man for the next millennium. But his father, Ralph, died at early age. And that has helped Dale Sr. focus on being a good father.

Junior is one of three Earnhardt children, all of whom say they grew closer to their dad as they became an adults.

"We've always been close," Dale says

lar to his father's ride in the mid-1980s, including the car in which Dad made his famous "Pass in the Grass" in 1987.

"I can remember as a little kid watching Dad drive the Wrangler Monte Carlo," Junior says, "and I always told myself I wanted to be in his shoes. In a way, watching that Wrangler car inspired me to pursue a career as a driver.

"So it's always had a special place in my mind. It's a big deal for me to drive a current-day version of the car that had such an impact on me as a child."

Junior won his 1998 title in the same No. 3 AC Delco car that his father occasionally raced on the Busch circuit. Then Junior made his Winston Cup debut in a Chevy with the No. 8, the number his grandfather carried for most of his career.

"I think all kids have the need to make their parents proud after all they do for us," Junior says. "Since I've been racing, all that runs through my mind is taking the chance and racing as best I can.

"I hope I have made my old man proud. When I win races, it puts a smile on his face. I don't care much about anything else, as far as the bonuses that come along with winning — the money, the exposure, the fame or what not.

"It's all just to make him happy. He's my daddy, and I love him to death."

of his namesake. "But the last few years we've been able to get even closer, because we've just gotten more opportunities to see each other.

"He lives right next to the shop and he's around all the time now. Plus, we spend most of our weekends at the same race track."

Junior entered his first Busch races with sponsorship from Wrangler Jeans. He drove a car with a paint scheme simi-

ntil 1999 when Roberto Alomar left the Orioles for the Indians, he and Sandy had played together 16 times in their professional careers, including six All-Star games. Their previous stint together occurred way back in 1989 with the San Diego Padres, whose coaching staff included their father, Sandy Sr. With 15 All-Star appearances between them before their reunion, the Alomar brothers are one of the most successful brother tandems is major league history. Their dad played 15 years in the majors, making for 35 years (and counting) of combined major league service for the family.

With football as the hot topic at the dinner table for almost four decades, it's not surprising that Florida State head coach Bobby Bowden has seen most of his sons follow him down the same career path. The oldest son, Steve, is a financial planner and the only non-coach of the group. Next in age is Tommy, who led Tulane to an unbeaten season in 1998 before taking the head coaching job at Clemson. Following him is Terry, who began his tenure at Auburn in 1993 with a 20-0 mark, becoming the first Division I-A coach to achieve such a feat. The youngest and newest Bowden to the coaching ranks is Jeff, who joined his father's staff in 1994 as receivers coach.

When Brian Griese ran off the field in celebration of leading the Michigan to their first national championship in 49 years, he ran into his father Bob Griese, a pretty good quarterback himself and lead analyst for ABC's college football telecasts.

A member of the Pro Football Hall of Fame, Brian's dad led the Miami Dolphins in 1972 to the NFL's last perfect season, and in 1997 saw his son lead the Wolverines to their first perfect season in 50 years. Brian became the Denver Broncos' third-round pick in 1998 and is waiting in the wings to replace HOF-bound quarterback John Elway.

obby Hull, the Golden Jet, is the greatest scoring left-winger in the history of frozen water.

Amazingly, son Brett Hull, the Golden Brett, ranks among the greatest scoring right wingers in hockey history.

They are the only father-son tandem to crack the 500-goal barrier. And for Brett Hull, the groundwork was laid when his dad jumped from the Chicago Blackhawks of the NHL to the Winnipeg Jets of the World Hockey Association.

"I don't know if I even skated back then when we were in Chicago," Brett says. "When we got to Winnipeg, the switch went on. That was like '71 or '72, so I was 5 or 6 years old. We were always skating before practice, after practice, on the weekends. My three brothers and me, because we were Bobby Hull's sons, we used to get away with murder.

The elder Hull was always willing to stick around late after games signing autographs, which gave his son even more ice time to play around with.

"After games we'd go out and skate and have the time of our lives," Brett says. "He'd shower and get dressed and go to the 'Wives Room' for a sandwich, and then stand there and sign like 500 autographs. So I'd be out on the ice forever with my brothers and their friends.

"Carey Wilson, who played with the

Flames later on, and his twin brother Jeff were my brother Blake's age. And their older brother Jerry was the same age as my brother Bobby. Their dad, Dr. Wilson, was the team doctor in Winnipeg, so his boys would always be around there, too. I was younger than all of them, but I could shoot it better than they could. But that's all I could do better."

The whole experience may have seemed like a lark, but Brett was starting down the same path as his Hall of Fame father. The experience of hanging out in a locker room full of professional hockey players turned out to be invaluable.

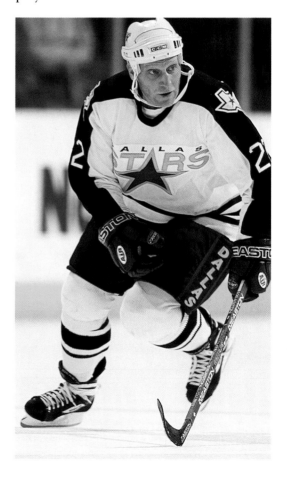

Hall of Famer Bobby Hull won seven goal-scoring titles and two NHL MVP awards in the 1960s. He and his son Brett are the only father-son combination to win the Hart Trophy and the only pair to score 500 goals each.

"You're understanding the game and the players and how they get themselves ready," Brett says.

"What a great way to get your start. We weren't just screwing around with skates and sticks and helmets, like the other kids. Our sticks were professional patterns cut to our length. The experience was unbelievable."

Bobby Hull also put his sons to work. They'd tape sticks and, in the days before high-tech sports drinks, pass around orange slices that the players would eat for energy before games.

But Bobby, a gruff Canadian farm boy, didn't force his sons into his footsteps.

"He was never the guy to take us onto the ice and say, 'Come on, you take a wrist shot like this,' " Brett says. "He'd just say, 'Watch and learn. When my line goes on the ice, see how we pass the puck? See how we set up a shot? Pay attention.' He didn't pat us on the head. If anything, he'd

kick us on the butt and tell you to get skating. That was his thing. And I never could skate like he could."

Brett's parents divorced during the Winnipeg years, and the children stayed with their mother, Joanne Robinson. When Brett became an adult, he and his father rebuilt their relationship, with hockey as the glue. They are extremely close now. "Big Bob," as Brett's wife Alison calls Bobby, gets a kick out of his grandchildren: Jude, Jayde and Crosby Hull.

And hockey still connects the Golden Jet with the Golden Brett, even though the son chose to sign with the Dallas Stars rather than dad's old Blackhawks.

"When we're on the phone or he comes to visit," Brett says, "you want to talk about the game, and what's going on with your line, and why you're not scoring. The great thing is, this guy knows exactly what you're talking about. He's been through exactly the same thing. Whether his philosophy's different or not, he can help you out. And his basic philosophy is the same as mine. We don't love playing defense, but we know it's an important part of the game.

"People say, 'Wasn't it a lot of pressure having Bobby Hull as your dad?' Are you kidding? I got to do more things and have more fun around a hockey rink. What other kid had that advantage?"

"Being a coach's son has helped me in so many ways — physically, mentally, technique-wise. My dad is my best friend, my confidante."

— *John Elway*

"Diabetes never slowed (my son) down. I don't think I had anything to do with that."

— *Jackie Smith*

MENTOR

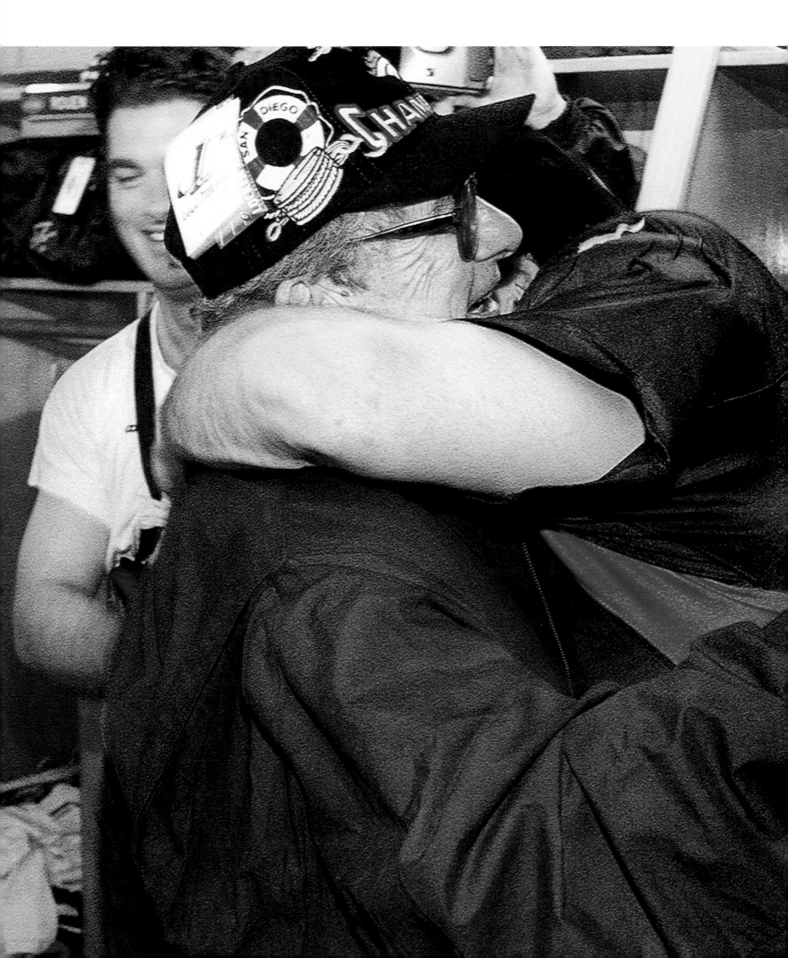

A nine-time Pro Bowler, John Elway shares his triumphs with Jack, his dad and former coach. John reached new heights in 1998, surpassing 50,000 career passing yards and claiming MVP honors in Denver's second straight Super Bowl victory.

During his odyssey as a college football coach, Jack Elway assembled some memorable teams from the raw material of youth. But he created his ultimate masterpiece in his own backyard.

John Elway's father taught him how to pass and run and lead a team, as well as how to hit a baseball and shoot a basketball. In the process, Jack and his only son became best buddies. Family members still chuckle at the memories:

• Jack and John on a baseball field on a hot August afternoon, exchanging horsehide tales and ancient banter.

• John standing on a rain-drenched sideline, watching his father conduct a University of Montana practice.

• Jack teaching 7-year-old John the mechanics of throwing a football, and John spending hours mastering those techniques.

• John passionately begging his father not to quit a one-on-one basketball game as night fell. "One more," the boy said. "One more."

Even John's first football game was telling. Jack, who arrived after halftime, asked Montana basketball coach Jud Heathcote how John was faring.

"Well," says Heathcote, who later coached Magic Johnson at Michigan State, "either every kid on that field is the worst football player I've ever seen, or your boy is the greatest player I've ever seen."

Young John had run for four touchdowns in the first half.

"My favorite player was Calvin Hill," John says. "I went around calling myself Calvin Elway."

Jack Elway wisely convinced his son to become a quarterback. In fact, the elder Elway made all the right moves. He started John in kindergarten a year later than normal so he'd have a better developed body by high school.

When John picked up a plastic bat and assumed his natural right-handed stance, Jack quickly converted him into a left-handed hitter in a preemptive move against curveballs.

Jack wouldn't let him ski in Montana's mountains, although his sisters were free to do so. And when Jack became Cal State-Northridge's head coach, he scouted the Los Angeles area for a high school with a high-tech passing attack.

John's high school career broke new ground. As a junior, he passed for 3,039 yards and led Granada Hills to the Los Angeles city playoffs. In a semifinal battle against San Fernando, John was unstoppable. But so was San Fernando's running game, which produced a 35-33 lead with a couple minutes left in the game.

John took over on Granada's 32, with

the weight of his team's season on his broad shoulders. Ad-libbing at the line of scrimmage, he quickly moved his team into scoring range. With 20 seconds left, he fired what appeared to be the winning touchdown pass.

It was called back, however, because of a holding penalty. So he re-loaded and threw another scoring strike.

"I wonder if he's as good as I think he is," Jack said to his wife after Granada's thrilling 40-35 win. "I wonder if John realizes how good he can be."

What John did realize — and savor — is his father's role in his life.

"My dad is the reason I'm what I am today," John says. "Being a coach's son has helped me in so many ways — physically, mentally, technique-wise. My dad is my best friend, my confidante.

"There have been many, many, many, many times I thought I was losing my sense of humor. It was so hard at times. But I always looked at it like it was something I wanted to pay the price for.

"I always went out and challenged myself to be as good as I can be. That's the way I was taught. He was always there when it got so tough. I could always talk to him."

oises Alou was first in 1998 NL MVP voting among players who didn't beat Roger Maris' home run record. Moises has shown many of the skills his father displayed during his 17-year career in the majors, but does Dad one better by being able to hit the ball out of the park.

The first Dominican-born manager in major league history, Felpe Alou had the opportunity to manage his son during six seasons at Montreal, before Moises signed with Florida and then Houston. Felipe has done well under difficult conditions. Since 1992 his Expos own the National League's third-best winning percentage with the league's lowest average payroll.

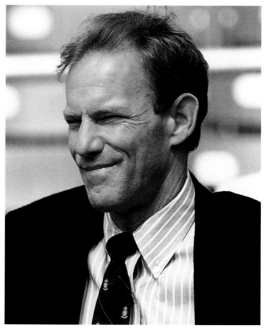

Ben Grieve, the 1997 AL Rookie of the Year, found out at an early age what it takes to play at the highest level. While his dad, Tom, was the General Manager of the Texas Rangers from 1984-'94, Ben spent time as the Rangers' batboy. They also made history together as the first father-son combination to be taken in the first round of the MLB draft. The Oakland Athletics selected Ben second over-all in 1994, and Tom was the first-round pick of the Washington Senators in 1966.

t all started innocently enough.

I purchased a couple of 1986 Topps baseball card packs at the local Target, although I don't even remember my motive for buying them.

I was just 8 years old, but it turned into one of the best investments I ever made, and not because of their collectible value. My dad found them lying around my room that winter, and by the next spring we were both full-blown baseball card addicts.

During the next four years, I would spend more time with my father than some less fortunate people do during their entire lives. Collecting baseball cards brought us together during my early teens, one of those tough periods during the development of the father-son relationship.

Looking back, I can't think of a better hobby for the two of us to have. Dad had collected baseball cards when he was a kid in the late '50s and early '60s. Collecting with me allowed him to relive an enjoyable part of his childhood. I was a baseball junkie. I grew up a fan of the St. Louis Cardinals and played Little League myself.

We definitely took collecting to an extreme.

It used to take the two of us 45 minutes to buy a gallon of milk from the convenience store a block away. We'd pick through every cellophane pack of cards in stock, trying to find rookie cards or All-Stars showing through the clear wrapper. In order to snag the best cards, we had the delivery schedule of the store timed so we could rummage through the packs the day they arrived. The cashier thought we were nuts.

We did more than just annoy convenience store clerks, though.

Eventually we started going to baseball card shows together, trying to get the newest cards or to pick up cards we needed to complete sets. After awhile we ended up selling cards at shows.

When Beckett was looking for a column written by a kid to capture the aspects of youth collecting, I ended up getting the job at age 9. The column was called Kids' Korner, and it ran for four years. My dad and I would get together once a month to write an article. I would dictate, and he would type it down and offer suggestions for improvement.

Finally, we made the ultimate collecting pilgrimage. We ended up driving to Dallas for the National Sports Collector's Convention. While we were there we got to tour the Beckett offices and the Score trading card company manufacturing plant.

Collecting allowed me to do a lot of other cool things. I got to be a batboy for a Cardinals game. I interviewed major league players for articles. People at college have asked me if I was the kid that wrote for *Beckett Baseball Card Monthly*. These are all things that don't usually happen to the average kid, and I had a blast doing them all.

However, the things I remember most about collecting are the little things I did with my dad, such as getting excited when we found that last card to complete a set. Or going through packs of cards at the store. Or lying on the floor with a ball game on the tube, sorting cards for hours at a time. Or arguing about which brand of cards had the best photos or designs. Or groaning when we found out how little our precious cardboard was really worth.

Dad and I don't collect cards anymore. Most of our collections are in boxes scattered throughout closets around the house. Every once in a while, though, we'll pull out a box or binder and flip through the cards.

It's fun to look back now at the players and brands that we liked. But it really isn't the cards that matter to us now. Even if they all disappeared tomorrow, it wouldn't matter.

They're only cardboard. Memories are forever.

Jackie Smith was the prototype tight end for the St. Louis Cardinals. He was big and strong and fast and tough, as likely to run over and drag a defender downfield as to run around him.

In fact, when he was inducted into the National Football League Hall of Fame, his average-per-catch ranked him ahead of several wide receivers enshrined in Canton, Ohio.

But this classic tough guy was a softy when it came to his own four children and sports. He refused to push them into athletics, although he was tickled when son Darrell and daughters Angie and Sheri became marathoners. Track and field, after all, is what earned Jackie a scholarship to college.

It was his youngest son, Greg, who decided to follow his father onto the football field. Despite developing diabetes as a youngster, Greg became an all-state running back in St. Louis, helping his team win a Missouri small schools championship.

Greg went on to play at the University of Missouri for two years. Then he transferred to Dartmouth University, where he helped his new teammates win an Ivy League title.

Jackie and his wife, Jeri, a former standout prep basketball player, supported their son. The hard-nosed Hall of Famer took particular care not to be an overbearing Little League dad.

"My relationship with my kids has never been one of pushing them into the thing," said Jackie, 59. "With Greg, he just asked me to go out and throw the football with him one day. He was about 10 years old. Shortly after that he was diagnosed with diabetes, but he wanted to take a look at the Little League football teams.

"So we went out and listened to the coach ranting and raving. Greg and I looked at each other and said, 'Nah!' So he played soccer and got pretty good at that. We were living in Arkansas then. When we moved up here to St. Louis, he went to John Burroughs School. He went out for football, and we didn't know how good he'd be.

"He just worked really hard. And he just did things on his own. My other kids did that, too, in their sports. I know Greg was much further ahead mentally than I was at that age."

Greg's can-do example was infectious with his teammates. Jackie made that point one day: "I told him, 'Greg, the guys look at you like a team leader. So if you get hurt, just try to get your treatment and not make a big deal of it. It might get them nervous or anxious.' So a few games later, on the first play of the game, he gets nailed pretty good. I could

A member of the Pro Football Hall of Fame, tight end Jackie Smith played in five Pro Bowls for the Cardinals. His son, Greg, was a running back for Dartmouth and helped lead the team to an undefeated season and an Ivy League title.

see he was unsettled a little bit when he carried the ball after that. He was not making sharp cuts like he usually did.

"Well, he was like that for the rest of the half. When they came out of the locker room for the second half, there's Greg on crutches. I went over to him and said, 'Greg, what happened?' And he said, 'I broke the outside bone on my leg on that first play. I heard that bone crunching, and I didn't want to let the guys see that I was hurt, but I just couldn't make myself go any more.'

"I said, 'Greg, that ain't what I'm talking about!'"

That was one of the few times father and son were not on the same page.

When Greg was uncomfortable with the situation at Missouri, Jackie did not try to nudge him back to that Division I-A team. He wholeheartedly supported the transfer to Dartmouth's less-glamorous, but academically more prestigious, program.

Dartmouth eventually won the title in the Division I-AA Ivy League. Jackie is more proud that Greg quickly won the respect of his new peers.

"Probably because of the diabetes," Jackie said, "he really liked tackling adversity. When it rained or was cold, he loved that. He said, 'Some of the guys slack off then. You can really have an advantage in a game with bad condi-

tions.' When he went up to Dartmouth, some of the players thought he was nuts. He'd be doing all the drills and smiling.

"He didn't look at it as hard work. He just enjoyed the experience very much. Then the kids voted him as one of the team captains both years he was there. At Dartmouth, there are no athletic scholarships. In that academic environment, the guys just play for the love of the game. I believe that's the best of both worlds. To me, that's what Greg was all about."

Jackie, a hurdler in high school, admired how Greg smoothly stepped past his physical affliction.

"Diabetes never slowed him down," Jackie said. "I don't think I had anything to do with that. I think Greg recognized on his own and felt on his own that this was a special time, the years he had playing football with your friends. He made the same type of friends at John Burroughs.

"To me, that's really the essence of sports, making friends that you'll have for life. To top it off, his senior year at Dartmouth, they had the only 10-game undefeated season they ever had. I was down on the field for the end of the Brown game, their big rival and the team they had to beat in the end to finish undefeated.

"It went down to the last play of the game. Dartmouth was ahead a few points,

and Greg had run the ball about 10 times in a row and made some first downs and ate up some time. Brown got the ball back and threw a pass that could have won the game, but Dartmouth ended up winning.

"Those Dartmouth kids just erupted. I don't remember ever getting that excited. That was such a goal of Greg's personally. He came up and hugged me and said, 'Dad, I don't know what I'm gonna do now!' I said, 'Well, you'll find somewhere else to put your effort.'"

Greg, now 24, works with older brother Darrell's video marketing business in California. Jackie keeps busy as a restaurateur, TV car pitchman and marketing official for a local casino.

The Hall-of-Fame dad has no regrets that his son did not follow his cleat-steps into pro football.

"My only gig was that Greg was happy at what he was doing," Jackie said. "And that we give him some type of guidance along the way. He always knew that it was just a special honor to be involved in a team sport. And so he made the most out of it every minute."

Like father, like son.

"(If) you have something you love, and your son found it and has that love of it too, and then you get to share it — it is just something special."

— *Kyle Petty*

"Let's just say that my vision of what it means to have daughters at home was inaccurate. I guess I saw my girls in dresses, with dolls and all that."

— *Dan Dierdorf*

FAMILY VALUES

Richard Petty dominated racing in the '60s and '70s, posting a record 200 wins. His son Kyle has eight Winston Cup victories, and his grandson Adam races in the NASCAR Busch series, making him the first fourth-generation athlete in any pro sport.

The Pettys believe the family that races together, stays together.

The family name is synonymous with stock car racing, with a Petty entered in almost every Winston Cup race in NASCAR's 50-year history. Four generations have competed in cars fielded by the family business, Petty Enterprises.

Lee Petty competed in the first NASCAR race in 1949, won the first Daytona 500 in 1959 and captured three Winston Cup championships. His son, Richard, earned the nickname "The King of Stock Cars" by setting records with 200 wins and seven Winston Cup champions.

Kyle, Richard's son, became the first third-generation driver to win a Winston Cup race and is still an active driver. Adam, Kyle's son, made sports history in 1998 when he became the first fourth-generation professional athlete in any sport. He won races on the ASA and ARCA circuits before advancing to the NASCAR Busch series in 1999.

Richard went to watch his dad compete in NASCAR's debut race as an 11-year-old tyke. He's been going to the races ever since, taking whatever family members who want to come along. "I don't even know any other way," Richard recalls. "My dad just took me and I just kept on going. When I started having kids, I just brought them with me as soon as they were old enough and wanted to come. I have grandkids hanging around the trailer now at every race."

Kyle started traveling to races with his dad during the summer after third grade. NASCAR was more of a barnstorming circuit then and the family spent most of the time on the road. During the races, Kyle would play in the infield with other drivers' sons.

But by the time Kyle had children, the circuit had changed. His wife and kids fly to the races on the weekends, with the youngsters of many of the drivers playing together and attending Sunday school classes in a trailer operated by MRO, a church-affiliated ministry.

The Pettys have lived and operated their race shop in the same rural community, near the towns of Level Cross and Randleman in North Carolina, since the end of World War II. Comforted by the familiar surroundings, Kyle didn't encounter many problems growing up as the son of a legend. He enjoyed the benefits, such as getting to see Evil Knievel jump and getting cool Knievel sunglasses, while suffering few drawbacks.

"The only time (my name) was a big deal to me is when I played football and basketball, and we went out of town," Kyle remembers. "You'd get a lot of cheap shots and late hits. All of that was just because they wanted to say the next day at school that they had done this to Richard Petty's son."

The trend of being the target of abuse continued when Kyle took up the family business of racing. That was one of the reasons why Kyle found himself with

a full-time family ride in Winston Cup when he was just a teenager. "We'd try the short tracks, but somebody from Joe's Service Station would take me out on the third lap just so that they could say that they took out the King's son," he recalls.

But Kyle had plenty of experience driving by that time. The Petty kids — both Richard's children and then Kyle's — usually got their first motorcycle by the time they were 6 or 7, and started driving cars on family property around age 10. It was nothing for them to drive on the state highway to the Petty shop, a trip of about two miles.

"My dad was really weird about go-carts because he thought they were dangerous," says Kyle, smiling at the irony of the situation. "We'd have motorcycles almost before we could walk. Then mom would send us to the shop when we were 10 to go pick up a case of Cokes. And so there we would be — driving a 1964 station wagon down the highway, forcing the police to follow us home because they were afraid

something would happen — yet we couldn't drive a go-cart."

Unlike his parents, Kyle let Adam and his other kids race go-carts, and it was then that he started to understand the concern his parents had felt when he started racing. "I had a totally different feeling about what my parents had gone through, especially my mother, when they let me race for the first time at Daytona even though I was just 18," Kyle explains. "For my mother, it was, 'Not only did I marry an idiot, but I raised an idiot.'"

Kyle did his share of worrying about the safety of his children, but in Adam's case, the concern quickly gave way to excitement. Kyle is proud of his son and believes he can be a great driver, if he can handle all the advice being offered by his relatives. As for watching his son

race, well, Kyle is thrilled beyond words.

"I don't think you can put it into words," Kyle says. "Unless you're a father and you have something you love, and your son found it and has that love of it too, and then you get to share it. It is just something special. I talk a lot, but I can't describe how great it is."

Adam understands, and he can't wait until a couple of decades from now when one of his kids becomes NASCAR's first fifth-generation driver.

"Getting to be one of the racing Pettys has been a dream of mine, an answer to my prayers," Adam says. "Racing is a family sport, and it brings everybody close together.

"I can't remember a time when I wasn't around a bunch of Pettys, and I can't remember when I wasn't around racing. It just all goes together."

With three generations of major leaguers, the Boone family has become intertwined in the fabric of baseball. The grandfather of the family, Ray, was an All-Star infielder during a 13-year big-league career from 1948 to 1960. Ray's son, ex-Royals skipper Bob Boone, is currently a senior adviser of player personnel in the Reds' organization and was a major league catcher for 19 years. Three of his sons still play the game today. Bret has taken his tough second base defense from Cincinnati to the Atlanta Braves. Aaron plays infield for the Reds, and the youngest, Matthew, plays in the Detroit Tiger farm system.

E ven with his six MVPs and six scoring championships with the Detroit Red Wings, Gordie Howe enjoyed no greater thrill than skating on the same team as his sons. In 1973, Gordie jumped at the opportunity join his sons, Mark and Marty, on the Houston Aeros of the WHA. For the 45-year-old dad it was a thrill of a lifetime. "Playing with my kids made it fun." Gordie won the MVP in the league and Mark was named Rookie of the Year. The three Howes led the Houston Aeros to WHA championships in 1974 and 1975, and they concluded their historic run together in 1979-80 with Hartford. Mark went on to skate for Philadelphia and Detroit, and Marty moved to the Bruins.

athers and their sporting daughters? Dan Dierdorf, the Hall of Fame offensive lineman and former colorful commentator on Monday Night Football, admits that the concept took some getting used to.

His three girls took the basketball court with a vengeance that surprised him.

"I didn't have any sisters when I was growing up," says Dan, who grew up in Columbus, Ohio, but stayed in St. Louis after his career ended with the Cardinals. "I had two brothers. Let's just say that my vision of what it means to have daughters at home was inaccurate. I guess I saw my girls in dresses, with dolls and all that.

"And that is a part of their lives. But my girls can get down and dirty and scratch and claw and compete as well as any boy. Boys and girls playing sports? There's no difference in my mind between the two.

They're fierce competitors."

It started with Kristen, who made the St. Louis Post-Dispatch All-Metro Team as a senior at Visitation Academy in 1989. She went to Michigan, her dad's alma mater, but opted not to play hoops.

Following in her sneakers are Dana, a 17-year-old junior last season at "Viz," and Katie, a 12-year-old seventh grader.

Dana, a 5-foot-8 forward/guard, was a varsity starter as a freshman and led the team in scoring in each of her first three

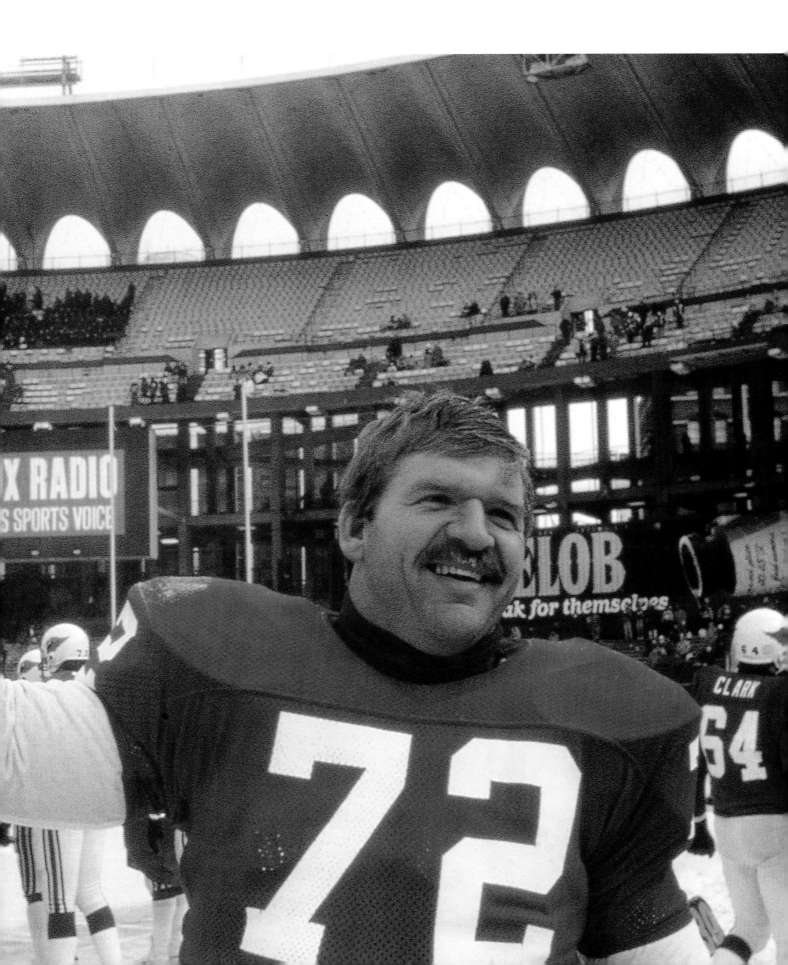

seasons. Katie, a 5-9 post player, is still growing and already a player to watch.

"I don't miss many games," Dan says. "I'll be the first to admit that I took it for granted, my mother and father being at the games. I had no sense that their stomachs were churning. You didn't think about that as a kid. I've had my share of thrills on the field. But my stomach is churning now when they play. Oh, I agonize."

That is not a complaint or proof that Dad expects great things from his daughters.

"I don't require my kids to play sports," Dan says. "I don't live vicariously through them. But I'm just thrilled that they're competing. (By playing sports) you learn a lot of different things about yourself and what it takes to compete. It sounds corny, I know, but sports teach you so much.

"Preparation. Focus. Having a passion about what you're doing. Those are all commodities that serve you well in life when you quit playing sports."

Organized sports offer another plus: Young athletes, male and female, are too busy and too tired at night to seek unhealthy adrenaline boosts.

"I never saw anyone smoking a cigarette or drinking a beer running up and down the court," Dan observes. "And I never saw anyone hanging around the shopping mall, getting ready for tip-off."

As a kid, Dan's sports were football, wrestling and track and field. His guiding principle applies to basketball, as well as any other activity.

When his girls first started bouncing a ball, Dan told them: "I really don't care if you play (on a team). But if you want to play, there are rules of engagement. You must play hard. Don't cheat yourself or anyone else you happen to be playing with by going at half speed."

Those rules of engagement still apply.

"I don't ask that. I demand that," he says. "They don't have to play.

But if you play, play it right. And they do. And that holds forth for basketball or English class or the debate team. Don't denigrate yourself and the sport. Don't go embarrassing yourself by not trying your best."

All three girls were willing disciples of their dad's Hall of Fame hustle. The rewards have extended well beyond the baseline.

"Just the sheer amount of time we've spent together has been tremendous," Dan says. "Both my younger girls play on national AAU teams, so we travel every summer to places like Shreveport, La., for tournaments. Last year, we went to New Orleans for eight days with Katie's 12-year-old team. And who's the head coach? Dana.

"The two girls are five years apart, a huge gap at their ages. What common interests can a 17-year-old can have with a 12-year-old? None. But you know something? Last summer, they did. And it was the best summer we ever had as a family."

To Dan's thinking, even bad times in sports have a good side.

"One thing that athletics teaches you is that there's no shame in losing," he says. "There's nothing wrong with trying as hard as you can and not winning and having to pick yourself up. You can't go through your life afraid to fail. Everybody does. You have to learn to keep going."

Dana, the middle one, is grappling with one of those trying situations.

"Dana is not nearly as tall as she thought she would be," Dan said. "Her little sister is already taller than her. So Dana's learning to play guard, when she was always a forward. It's just fate. It's nothing she did wrong. Hey, life's not fair. It's a wonderful lesson."

As for dad, every game is a refresher course in self-restraint.

"I get excited like anybody else," Dan says. "But I also have to realize that everybody in that gymnasium knows who I am. And everybody knows who my daughter is. So I can't yell at the officials. I can't do anything. I usually try to just sit there.

"I get mad and I get angry when my girls do something I don't like. So I mumble to my wife, who sits with me and puts up with that for a little bit, and then she moves. I don't applaud when somebody on the other team makes a mistake, because I know she's somebody's daughter, too."

Other fans are not as empathetic.

"Dana has been heckled in high school gyms," Dan says. "Some of the guys get together and start chanting her name. It's not easy for her, but it's the price you have to pay to be somebody's daughter. But my kids get a lot of nice perks, too. And Dana's mature enough to understand that."

This summer, Dan will be back in the bleachers, sometimes sitting through five or six games at a weekend tourney.

"Basketball has been a big part of our lives," Dan says. "Sports has been a real blessing for our family. I need somebody to tell me why that's a bad thing."

"I'm not against my kids idolizing other people because that means they see me as their father and really don't see me as a basketball player."

— *Michael Jordan*

"My mother doesn't just know me as a ballplayer. She knows me as a son. She knows everything about me — good, bad and indifferent."

— *Terrell Davis*

ROLE MODELS

After retiring in 1999, Michael Jordan has more time for his children (Jeffrey, Marcus and Jasmine) and his wife, Juanita. Michael led the NBA in scoring a record 10 times, was regular season MVP five times and Finals MVP six times.

t was the hottest rumor in pro hoops since, well, Carmen and Dennis. Was it possible that Michael Jordan actually decided to retire from basketball after his oldest son, Jeffrey, was heard to confess that Shaquille O'Neal - Shaq Daddy!? — was his favorite NBA player?

OK, what about it, daddy dearest?

"No, that's not true," Jordan insists. "But my middle kid loves Dennis Rodman and he wants red hair. I'm not against my kids idolizing other people because that means they see me as their father and really don't see me as a basketball player, and that means my wife and I are doing our jobs in terms of being the great parents that we have to be. So if they see other players as being like their idols, I don't have a problem with that."

For years, what the most famous father in sports had a problem with was the NBA time clock. Jordan always liked kids, especially his own, but quality family time was harder to come by than hair on his head. When you average three practices and three games and three plane trips and dozens of media interviews and business meetings per week, there isn't much time to spend with a wife, three kids and a golf game.

Know that picture of Jordan and his kids in a tub full of soap bubbles at the family mansion? Sure was warm and fuzzy,

all right. About as rare as an air ball in the final minute of a close game, too.

It's not that Jordan didn't understand the importance of family or anything like that. As a kid in Wilmington, N.C., his idea of a perfect day was three hours of basketball, lunch, three hours of basketball, dinner, three hours of basketball. When he wasn't playing basketball, he was playing baseball, his first love. If James Jordan hadn't been around to insist that the grass be cut and the dishes be washed, then his son would have pulled it off, too.

It was James Jordan — with an assist from Michael's mother, Deloris — who taught him the value of sweat, that life was more than a 15-foot jump shot on the family driveway.

"My heroes are and were my parents," Michael says to this day. "I can't imagine having anyone else as my heroes."

It wasn't long before James and Michael would become more than just a father and a son. They were the best of buds. The two traveled together. They played cards together. And, oh, how they laughed together. Then Michael heard the worst news possible one day in July 1993. His best friend had been shot dead alongside a country road in North Carolina.

Drawing from memories of his childhood, Michael used this father's advice as

inspiration during his NBA career and during his stint as a minor league ballplayer from 1993 to 1995. "Every morning, I talk to him," Michael explained at the time. "'Keep doing what you're doing,'" he'd tell me. Keep trying to make it happen. . . . Then he'd say something funny or recall something about when I was a boy when we'd be in the backyard playing catch together, like we did all the time."

The funny thing about life is, it has no timeouts, no seventh-inning stretch, no break in the action when a principal wage-earner — much less the world's most famous athlete — can spend, say, a year full-time teaching his kid how to hit

a curve ball. So Jordan started to think seriously about retirement even before one of his kids had allegedly sold out to the Shaq Diesel.

It wasn't the first time Jordan had considered a clear-out play for his family, but the last time it happened, in 1993, professional baseball got in the way. In January 1999, nearly six years and three more NBA titles later, Jeffrey, Marcus and Jasmine ranged from 3 to 7 years of age, an even better time for their father to watch and help them grow from a close distance. At 35, Jordan still was young enough to be a kid himself, wasn't he? Finally, he came to the conclusion that, at this stage of his life, a weekday night would be better spent with the family at home than against the Vancouver Grizzlies two time zones away.

His wife Juanita couldn't agree with him more. "I see Michael doing more car-pooling," she says.

On the morning of his retirement announcement, Jordan already was in Mr. Mom mode. "I enjoy taking my kids to school, which I did this morning," he said that day. "I enjoy picking my kids up from school, which I look forward to doing, and watching my kids play. My wife and I have a fun time watching our kids play one-on-one. Those are things that seem so simple in a lot of people's lives and never really have been enjoyed by me because of my schedule and because of the things that I've done over the last 14 years."

Heck, things already are different in the Jordan household.

"Just no red hair," daddy says.

lex Rodriguez has become one of the brightest stars in the majors, but he hasn't gotten there alone. The Mariners' 23-year-old shortstop was brought up by his mother in Miami, and to this day she plays a large part in his life. "There's no way would I have made it this far without her," says Alex, who in 1998 became just the third 40/40 (homers and stolen bases) man in major league history. "I confide in her and she has advice on every major decision I make, along with my sister and brother. She has a lot of wisdom. I'll never take her out of that role. I still talk to her three or four times a week."

*T*iger Woods, who attained the No. 1 world ranking at a younger age and quicker than any golfer in history, has always had strong ties to his mother, Kultida, and father, Earl. When he was very young, his mom would drive him to the golf course and driving range to let him do what he loved. "When he was 18 months old he would go to the driving range. When he was done hitting I'd put him back in the stroller and he'd fall asleep." Both she and Earl have always been there in rain or shine, and their support came to fruition in 1997 when Tiger claimed the season-opening Mercedes Championships, and three months later, shattered several records in winning the Masters.

ong considered the best golfer who had never won a major, Davis Love III claimed the 1997 PGA Championship with rainbows in the background. As he hugged his mother, Penta, he also thought of his father, who died in a 1998 plane crash. Davis III had spent countless hours talking and training with his best friend, his dad, and he had a feeling his father was there with him that moment. "Those two rainbows on 18 showed that he was sharing it with me. I'd like to think that was him and Harvey Penick up there watching."

eraldine Barber's twin sons, Tiki and Ronde, have often thrived together. The "Barbers of C'Ville," as they were nicknamed at Virginia, Tiki set the Virginia all-time rushing mark of 3,389 yards and Ronde was a three-time all-ACC cornerback. They both were drafted in 1997: Tiki to the Giants in the second round, and Ronde to the Buccaneers in the third.

Georgia Woodson stood by her son Charles when he was named winner of the 1997 Heisman Trophy at the Downtown Athletic Club in New York. From winning the national championship at Michigan to becoming the first defensive player ever to win the Heisman Trophy, Charles was red hot. And the NFL draft continued his streak. The Oakland Raiders drafted him No. 4 overall, and the cornerback claimed the NFL Defensive Rookie of the Year Award.

Leading the Denver Broncos two Super Bowl wins in as many years, Terrell Davis ran for more yards in 1998 (2,374 in the regular and postseason) than anyone in NFL history. The record he broke, 2,331 yards, was his own, set in 1997.

t was the morning after a 20-16 loss to the New York Giants, which had ended the Denver Broncos' hopes for a perfect 1998 season, and Terrell Davis was weary and bruised and fighting the flu.

So why was the NFL's leading rusher smiling?

Before coming to club headquarters, Davis had spent a couple hours with his mother, Kateree Davis, a bona fide triple-threat in her own right.

"Besides being my mother, she's my best friend and confidante," Terrell says.

Terrell has needed every bit of Kateree's help over the years. Before becoming the Broncos' go-to guy, before becoming an NFL star, and before becoming a national celebrity, his life as a kid in San Diego and later in college was a litany of trouble and setbacks that would have defeated a lesser person.

• Eighteen years ago, Terrell's father, Joe, came home one night, awakened four of his five sons, then made them stand against a bedroom wall. To see how "tough" they were, he took out a .38-caliber pistol, aimed and fired a bullet over each son's head. The boys could feel the whoosh of the bullets.

• Awhile later, Terrell's father and Kateree's cousin got into a fight with a friend. The friend left, picked up a shotgun at his house, returned to Terrell's house

111

and started firing. Terrell's father and Kateree's cousin returned fire.

Terrell, the youngest son, slept through the gun battle in a nearby bedroom before being awakened by a policeman's flashlight. He was 9.

• Beginning at age 7, Terrell was tormented by periodic migraine headaches. They incapacitated him and even pushed him to the brink of suicide. "I'd rather be dead,"he would tell himself. "I don't want to live. I can't stand the pain."

• In 1987, when Terrell was 14, Joe Davis died of lupus, an autoimmune disease. He had refused to take his medication.

When his father died, part of Terrell did, too. "I never thought my dad could go that way," Terrell recalls. "I was devastated when that day came."

The entire family took a hard hit, but the mother, Kateree, was there to pick up the pieces.

"Everybody kind of went into a shell," she explains. "It was like you didn't know where you were. I was worried about all of (my kids)."

The youngest child found solace in his daily routine. He showed up at school and football practice on time and showing no signs of anguish over his loss. Terrell's morning began at 5 a.m., with a paper route he refused to abandon even during his darkest days.

"He never complained," his mother recalls. "He just got up, did his newspapers, then went to school. Sometimes, I'd get up and help him. That way he could sleep a little (later)."

• In 1991 his brother, Bobby, was charged with murder after shooting a pregnant woman in the chest during a robbery attempt. The woman survived, but the five-month-old baby she was carrying inside of her was killed.

In a landmark case that changed California law, Bobby was found guilty of the murder of a fetus.

• After one season at Long Beach (Calif.) State, Terrell learned the football program had been abruptly terminated. Davis transferred to Georgia, where, during his final season, a leg injury limited his effectiveness and caused head coach Ray Goff and Bulldog fans to turn on him.

They expected Davis to carry the load as had the likes of Herschel Walker and Garrison Hearst, but he wasn't fully healthy until the final few games of the season. Projected as a second- or third-round draft pick entering the season, he tumbled into NFL obscurity, the sixth round of the 1995 draft to the eager Broncos.

Any one of those traumas might have knocked a young person off course.

Through all the mad and bad times, Terrell never lost his faith in the future — thanks to his mother, who now lives in Denver to be near her youngest son.

"She's been there since Day One," says Terrell, who in 1998 became just the fourth NFL player ever to rush for 2,000 yards (2,008). "My mother doesn't just know me as a ballplayer. She knows me as a son. She knows everything about me — good, bad and indifferent.

"She's always tried to direct me in the right direction. And for that, she's my role model. She's a remarkable person."

"How many kids can say they had their dreams come true, much less playing in the same big-league game side-by-side with their dad?"

— *Ken Griffey Jr.*

"I see things in (Dougie's) eyes and his facial expressions that no one else sees."

— *Doug Flutie*

MAGIC MOMENTS

When you ask Ken Griffey Jr. what part of his outstanding baseball career means most to him, his answer might surprise you unless you know the real Junior.

Of all the star center fielder's glittery accomplishments, his fondest memory has nothing to do with All-Star games or back-to-back 56-homer seasons.

"The best time I ever had in baseball was playing in the same outfield as my father," he says. "It was my dream growing up. How many kids can say they had their dreams come true, much less playing in the same big-league game side-by-side with their dad?

"I'm the only one and nothing can top that."

The response is as forceful as The Griffey Swing.

While Junior is best known as a ballplayer whose intensity is sometimes masked by his effortless skill and 1,000-watt smile, his personal focus is as a son to Ken Sr. and Birdie Griffey, as an older brother to Craig and, in more recent years, as husband to Melissa and father to son Trey, 5, and daughter Tarin, 3.

"When baseball is such a big part of several lives in one family, sometimes the lines get blurred and the game becomes part of family life," says Ken Sr., a superb outfielder and three-time All-Star in his own 19-year big-league career.

In 1989, Ken Griffey Sr. and Ken Jr. became the first father-son combination to play in the major leagues at the same time. And in 1990, they added two more family records by playing in the same lineup (Mariners) and homering in the same game.

117

"You try to separate the job aspect from the enjoyment of the sport, but there's no denying that baseball is a major part of your existence.

"Now, take that times three."

By three, Ken Sr. means himself, Junior and Craig. An athlete of note in his own right, Craig concentrated on football as a defensive back at Ohio State until the Mariners tightened their links to the family and made him a 42nd-round pick in the 1991 June draft. While Craig didn't experience the success on the diamond he might have had on the gridiron, the lure of joining father and brother in the game was too strong to resist.

Little wonder. The Griffeys are a unique and amazing story in baseball.

"What it took was two special and gifted people and players," says Lou Piniella, who played with and managed Ken Sr. and currently coaches Junior. "I can't even begin to think when you might see all the factors combine for us to see it again."

Similar as players, Ken Sr. and Junior are also quite alike as people. The sameness was evident from the first time Junior took batting practice in Seattle's Kingdome.

"You see Junior hit and you'd swear you were watching his old man swing the bat," says Bob Harrison, the senior scout who signed Junior for Seattle. "They are

alike, although Junior might have more bat speed."

Ken Sr. knew The Griffey Swing would be part of his son's abilities from the start.

"I first saw both the ability to adjust and the concentration level long before Kenny got to the majors. I saw it when he was a kid, about 12 or 13, and I was his batting-practice pitcher.

"I would throw him sliders, curveballs, forkballs, screwballs, change-ups. It didn't matter. He would make the adjustments. That's when I knew he was going to be a good player.

"It was important to see those things then, to have that knowledge, because shortly after (that) my career took me away from the Reds and Cincinnati, where Kenny, Craig, my wife Birdie and I (lived). I didn't get to see him play from 12 to 17. I didn't get to see him develop."

What he missed was a replay of his childhood, as Junior blossomed into a mirror image of his old man with a few refinements: Junior hits more homers and is a slightly better fielder. Yet, the swings match, as do their personalities. Before their first game together, against Detroit in Seattle on Aug. 31, 1990, Junior told his agent, Brian Goldberg, "It's really going to be weird tonight, playing with my dad."

Later, when Goldberg was driving Ken Sr. to the game, the father said, "It's really going to be weird tonight, playing with my son."

Both are easygoing and quick to laugh. Both have a serious streak, too, but they're better known for the shared sense of humor.

The humor was evident even in that historic first game. They started off by hitting back-to-back singles off the Tigers' Storm Davis, then Ken Sr. later had to make several long running catches in left. As his father jogged back to his position, Junior put his face behind his glove but his shaking shoulders betrayed his laughter.

Yet both had poignant thoughts on that first game they shared.

"When we went into the first to start the game, I didn't know what to think," Junior says. "I wanted to cry or something. It just seemed like a father-son game, like we were out in the backyard again just playing catch. But we were actually in a real game. I just stood there and looked at him. A couple of pitches even went by; I didn't watch."

"I didn't know what to expect," Ken Sr. remembers. "The first time up was like being a rookie again. But after the first pitch, I settled down."

The two had a bet — for dinner — on who would get the first hit. When

Junior followed his dad's single with one of his own, he called it a tie.

They displayed the best example of their friendly rivalry when they blasted historic back-to-back homers on Sept. 14, 1990.

Ken Sr. had homered in two previous games, but both times Junior had failed to follow up. That night at Anaheim against the Angels, after his dad homered, Junior greeted him at home plate and didn't say a word.

"I could see it in his eyes," Ken Sr. recalls. "I felt for him then. I knew he would be thinking home run. I hit the first two against Oakland and Boston, and I knew he had tried hard to hit one, too. Maybe too hard.

"I just sat quiet in the dugout and hoped he got a pitch he could hit, then . . . boom."

Most of the Mariners climbed to the top of the dugout steps to greet Junior, but Ken Sr. stayed behind, clapping, proud as any father could be.

"He was the first person I looked for," Junior says.

When the son got into the dugout, they looked at each other, smiled and embraced. Then the famous Griffey humor kicked in.

"It's about time," Ken Sr. told his son.

What is little known is that Ken Sr., at 40, outhit his son that final month of the 1990 season, .400 to .312, including a 12-game hitting streak. The two shared just 15 games that year and 30 games in 1991 before Ken Sr. retired.

"(Playing with Junior) tops my career, better than the '76 batting race (he finished second), even better than two World Series," Ken Sr. says. "(That), for me, is No. 1."

When Barry Bonds was just 4 years old, his mother, Pat, would drive him and his brother, Rickey, to Candlestick Park, where they'd shag flies and run free in the Giants' clubhouse. Hanging around dad's office must have worked, as Barry and his father, Bobby, hold the all-time father-son home run (743), RBI (2,240) and stolen base (906) career records. They're also the only two major leaguers with five seasons of more than 30 home runs and 30 stolen bases.

Don Shula set an NFL record with 347 victories in 33 seasons and guided the Miami Dolphins to Super Bowl titles after the 1972 and 1973 seasons. His son Dave became the youngest NFL head coach in the modern era at 32 when the Cincinnati Bengals hired him in 1991. They combined to make the record book twice more, when the Bengals met the Dolphins in the only two father-son head coaching match-ups in NFL history.

Doug Flutie will never know the pride and joy of watching his son, Doug Jr., follow in his distinguished football cleat prints.

The Buffalo Bills' quarterback and 1984 Heisman Trophy winner will never see Dougie play organized basketball. Or baseball. Or soccer. Or any other sport.

Father and son will not bond by playing catch in the backyard or by watching games together on television or in person.

Seven-year-old Dougie Jr. is autistic. Pride and joy for his father is just making even the tiniest connection with his son through eye contact and facial expressions.

"I see things in his eyes and his facial expressions that no one else sees," Doug says. "One night, I was sitting on the bed and I grabbed him, turned, caught great eye contact with him and said, 'Say, Hi, to Daddy.'

"And he wanted to. I saw it in his eyes . . . and nothing came out. When I walk into a room and he turns his head, no one else might even acknowledge it as a smile. But I see the smile, and I see the eye contact, and he's excited.

"He just doesn't know what to do, so he might shake a little bit. But I see it."

Five weeks into the 1998 season, Doug quickly became the toast of Buffalo. He replaced injured Rob Johnson and led the Bills to the playoffs. For his efforts, he became the oldest "rookie" named to the Pro Bowl squad.

At age 36, he has recaptured the national spotlight he gained with one of the most famous sports plays in history — his Hail Mary pass to give Boston College a mammoth upset over the University of Miami in 1984.

But he is also a husband and a father. And when he thinks of Dougie Jr. and 10-year-old daughter Alexa, games and money and fame don't seem to matter all that much.

"Dougie puts things in perspective for me," Doug explains. "People get so carried away with how important this game is. And it's important to me, or I wouldn't be playing it. But it's not life and death.

"Ten years from now, who's going to remember a certain game we played? Ten years from now, there's Dougie turning 17. Will he be able to get himself dressed in the morning?"

Until age 3, Dougie was a healthy child. Then, all of a sudden, he lapsed into an autistic shell and stopped talking. Doctors believe he will probably never speak.

During the season, Doug's wife, Laurie, and children live in Boston. Before signing with the Bills as a free agent in January, Doug kept his family with him in his eight seasons in the Canadian Football League. That togeth-

Doug Flutie started for the Buffalo Bills in 1998, his first NFL start since 1989 and the second-longest hiatus in league history. Named to the Pro Bowl in first year back, Flutie had captured six CFL Most Outstanding Player awards.

erness is no longer possible since Dougie became ill and needed constant care. So Doug flies his wife and children to every Buffalo home game, then returns to Boston whenever possible on off days.

Dougie attends a public school with a private program for autistic children. He also receives tutoring at home two to three hours per day after school and on weekends.

Despite all going against them, father and son have one athletic moment they can share. Doug sits behind Dougie in the hallway of their home, their legs spread, and helps the boy roll a ball back and forth with his mother.

"I don't know if he'll ever talk," Laurie says, "but we don't focus on that. We just take it day by day, step by step."

Editor's Note: Part of Doug Flutie's motivation for returning to the NFL was to help raise awareness about his son's disorder. He and his wife, Laurie, founded the Doug Flutie Jr. Foundation for Autism. It is part of The Giving Back Fund, a national nonprofit organization that creates and manages charitable foundations for athletes, entertainers and others. Some proceeds of "Flutie Flakes," a breakfast cereal that Doug introduced last October, go to the foundation. So does a portion of the cost of dialing 10-10-220 for long-distance telephone calls.

CONTRIBUTORS

Design by Sara Maneval

Front Cover Photos

Manny Millan (Hills)
V.J. Lovero (McGwires)

Photography

ALLSPORT USA
Craig Jones
Andy Lyond
Otto Gruele
Damian Strohmeyer
Jed Jacobsohn
Rick Stewart
Ken Levine
Chris Cassidy
Jamie Squire
B. Muscolino
Vincent Laforet
Stephen Dunn
David Taylor
J. Rettaliata
Doug Pensinger
Lonnie Major
Elsa Hasch
Jose L. Marin
Tom Hauck
Jonathan Daniel
Ezra O. Shaw
Kirk Schlea

AP Wide World Photos

Arlington Morning News

BRUCE BENNETT STUDIOS
B. Bennett
M. DiaGiacom
Brian Winkler

TOM DIPACE
PHOTOGRAPHY
Tom DiPace
DeHoog/TDP

David Drapkin/Sports
Imagery

Harold Hinson

Ken Kerr/Toronto Sun

MAJOR LEAGUE BASEBALL
Jeff Carlick
Scott Wachter
Tim Parker
John Reid III

NBA PHOTOS
Greg Shamus
Andrew D. Bernstein
Randy Belice
Nathaniel S. Butler
Andy Hayt

NFL PHOTOS
Herb Weitman
David Drapkin
James Flores
Darryl Norenberg

THE STOCK MARKET
Jose L. Pelaez
Ariel Skelley
Pete Saloutos
R.B. Studio
Ed Bock
Steve Prezant
John Welzenbach
John Henley
Chuck Savage

OUTLINE
Marc Royce
Gregory Heisler
Davis Factor

SPORTS ILLUSTRATED
V.J. Lovero
Manny Millan
Patrick Murphy-Racey
Doug Pensinger
Jerry Wachter

Ron Vesely Photography

Writers

Kevin Sherrington, author of the Introduction, is a sports feature writer for The Dallas Morning News. His work has appeared in The Best American Sports Writing 1991 and Best Newspaper Writing 1996. He and his wife, Debbie, have four children: Jake, Madeleine, Ford and Olivia.

Brian Allee-Walsh is the national NFL writer for the New Orleans Times-Picayune.

Vic Carucci covers the Bills for the Buffalo News.

Bob Finnigan covers the Mariners for the Seattle Times.

Paul Ladewski is the Chicago Bulls beat writer for the Daily Southtown Economist.

Clay Latimer covers the Denver Nuggets and Broncos for The Rocky Mountain News.

Chris McCosky is the Pistons beat writer for The Detroit News.

Tom Wheatley is a sports columnist and feature writer for the St. Louis Post Dispatch.

Tommy Wheatley, Tom's son, is an honor student at Truman State University in Kirksville, Mo., majoring in communications.

Mark Zeske is a senior editor for Beckett Publications.